Lucy Cleveland

The Scarlet-Veined and Other Poems

Lucy Cleveland

The Scarlet-Veined and Other Poems

ISBN/EAN: 9783744646406

Printed in Europe, USA, Canada, Australia, Japan

Cover: Foto ©Thomas Meinert / pixelio.de

More available books at **www.hansebooks.com**

THE SCARLET-VEINED

And Other Poems

BY

LUCY CLEVELAND

AUTHOR OF

"Lotus Life and other Poems," "The Dog of the Old Guard,"
"My Lady's Strange Girdle," etc.

NEW YORK
A. D. F. RANDOLPH COMPANY
103 FIFTH AVENUE
1897

Composition and Presswork by
M., W, & C. Pennypacker.

CONTENTS.

CONTENTS.

IV.

POEMS OF NATURE:

CONTENTS.

THE SCARLET-VEINED.

To

The Supreme Poet.

O Thou who o'er the chasm's ink
Of the abyssmal Void didst move
In rhythmic breathings; on the brink
Of the song-worlds all Life all Love
Were Thine, O burning heart of the o'er-
brooding Dove !

O my Scarlet-Veined a-fluttering and a-kin to
God's great azure,
Stretching strongly, strangely, sternly to dawn,
to dusk to-day,
Within each palm an ocean, and the sun itself
obeisant
In crimson beaker pledging, ere it laughs at
old Bombay;
The stars are trooping, envious, over tosses of
veined oceans
To anchor in thy lightnings, and to hearken
at thy knees,
O my Standard, stand thou strong and worthy,
worthier yet, a beacon
Against God's upper azure to the darkening
dynasties!

The Scarlet=Veined.

December 25th, 1776.

THE day was ebbing slow into that Vast
   That spreads its arms, a sudden darken-
      ing blur
Like an o'ersweeping wave of eagle's wing
Around an hour moving towards the dusk
To pass into the Night, from whose great breast
Beating with blood of stars it shall arise
New-voiced, fed with a meteor's battle-breath
Of utterance prophetic hurled from heaven
To startle nations and illume a world.

The night is needful for the mellowing
Of all great purpose.

13

On the camp it lies,
The silent outposts on the Delaware
Where a young nation waited for a morn.
The river glances with dread gleam, a white
That curdles through the silence, and strikes
    chill
Upon the threshold of the valiant hearts
That watch beside her waters' corpse-like calm,
Her speechless lips that part, but speak no
    word,
Her long gray spectre-face—Is it the ghost
Of years to come, come Now? The spectre-form
Of a great people's hopes doomed in this night
To die? Will that dread ghastliness arise
In sheeted horror that dries up the blood
Of e'en the boldest in the van of life,
And calls men's eyeballs out. Moving it comes,
Moving a-down the night, this sheeted Dead,
Its long bleached finger of dread bone out-
    stretched,

Still looming awful, e'en above the pine
That holds the rim of moonlight.   The dread
   White
Smiles.   And the smile's more hideous than a
   curse.
The finger beckons to arise and come.
The long and long perspective of stacked guns
Seem, in this gray chill mist, to move and move
A ghostly caravan of corpses dread
Across the leagues of distance, a grim band
Whose bones are whiter than the moon's amaze
That crept and searched along the ground last
   night,
And quick withdrew, with lips of horror pale,
Behind a gibbous cloud that bulged to laugh
With swollen cheeks at the lean band of men
Who plan to plant a nation now, and turn
Thy plethoric scorn, O Britain ! on thyself.

The bivouac at midnight of the men

Who, from the wasted troops, have mustered
  grit
In grasp of one staunch purpose : To plough
  through
The ice of obstacle, yea, and to meet
Great Death himself, and from his hideous hand
Wrest the dread scythe and wield it in dread war.

'Tis bivouac at midnight.   The low wind
Sways the black straps upon the cartridge-box
That's hung upon the sword ; and that's the
  Cross.
It's planted firm, and watches dauntless souls.
God moves, the Infinite's Humanity,
Towards the magnet irresistible—
Great men.   To-night you'll trace the word
  they wrote
Across the snow's long ghastly chronicle
(Death's mirror).   From their worn feet drop-
  ped blood

As on and on they marched, yea, though a
    Gates
Has turned his back on danger, duty; yea,
Though a Wilkinson's from Bristol fled,
Yea, though a Griffin who should plant his grip
Of iron mould, that sudden spurts in fire,
Within the flesh of the great enemy—
Yea, though these men have fled the surge
That mounts in fiery foam along our lines—
Terraced on terror, lo! they sit aloof
From this night's wave of opportunity,
Yet the great heroes marched. Heroes sublime,
What bell will ring to ages your great shout?
Heroes sublime, I envy ye that Night.
Ye planted the red seed we reap to-day
In golden harvest on our land's lit soil.
That blood has moistened history's old face
Flushed with new life this pregnant Christmas
    night,
As when, along the old Judea-roads,

The light from Joseph's lantern dropped red
   flecks,
A drip of blood along the moonlight snow,
As slowly with pained feet he plods along
And holds the lantern high to illume the face
Of her who'll bear the Christ in Bethlehem's
   cave.
Christ's hazard-road is marked with flecks of
   blood.
Thus must it ever be, O signal soul !
'Tis greater, verily, to sow the seed
Of all a grand Hereafter, yea, in start
Of muscles' giant agony, than to sit
In sun-crowned plenty yellowing all the fields.
Whose is the crown when God's voice calls
   the Roll ?

Darkness upon our forces.   There's no hint
Of the great shout when the great sky caught
   fire,

And *Gloria in Excelsis* to the Lord
Rushed like the roseate stream from opal-wings
Of the great Cherubim.

               The night shuts down;
No standard has this nation save the light
That gleams in great men's eyes, like planets'
    fires
When the pall'd clouds part on the acres vast,
And the great purpose of Immensity
Writes its star-alphabet of record down.
But night is needful for the mellowing
Of their great purpose.   They are veterans.
Their veins are Puritan.   Their muscles bred
To hoist new standards o'er an ocean's toss;
Sinews of granite, carved from out thy hills,
O thou New England! nurse and mother dear,
Who from thy breast's milk mad'st the men
To cleave a path through the Impossible,
To open shining doors for shuddering slaves.

THE SCARLET-VEINED.

Though France hold back, and Philadelphia
    fall,
New England will hold on—and climb by knee,
By fist, by teeth, and grapple up the slope.
Yea, though this very night she meet and close
With those imposing massive lines of men
Haloed with steel, a bayonet-torrent broad
That sweeps with irresistible smooth swirl
And levels e'en the mightiest. Britain, thou,
Thy haze of giant faces, foam of plumes,
Thou hurricane of valor round a world!

But Pennsylvania's woods send forth her men
Who stand as solid as her beechen trees
Down this supreme of storm. Yea, Hand is here,
And holds in giant palm his veterans
He'll dash upon thine outposts, Britain, soon.
Virginia, too, at whom colonial lips
Have sometimes curled: "She breeds but court-
    iers,

Who're warm (in wooing); skill'd in handling, fine,

The perfumed fans of ladies.   Courtiers

Who're busy with grave cares (that make them stoop)

For their knee-buckles.   Cavaliers, you see.''

''You see.''—What see you near the Delaware?

The ''velvet'' of good blood dyes the strong limbs,

The ''shapely'' limbs of Old Virginia's sons,

Its signet on their signal march to-night.

The powder of God's storm, the ice-wind's lace

Trims their rent clothes.   Their naked feet grasp ground,

And wrest it, thus, for all the ages' gaze—

These ''cavaliers'' along the Delaware.

This ''Cavalier'' along the Delaware—

Who is that man who walks alone, out there,

Beyond the distant edge of bayonet-gleam?

Quarried from out the black he looms erect,

The black of care, of disappointment, loss—

A silhouette against the rocks of chance,

The crystal strong that gathers to its breast

The colored leaps of fire from out the dark

And binds them for a torch unto a people.

Quarried from out the strain of all the life

Lived in the open 'neath God's lamps alone,

Inured to hardship, bivouac, to risk,

To self-dependence midst the fiery wreath

Of savage eyes.   Thus, the man's made.   He

    stands,

A silhouette against an old world's smile:

"George the Surveyor!" sneered the English lip

As it "surveyed" its George-phylacteries

Of kingly bulk.   Has it "surveyed" with care?

Methinks that ermine sweepeth leprously,

Its silken rustle cried "Unclean, Unclean!"

"George the Surveyor!" Let's consult a Book:

THE SCARLET-VEINED.

One Adam's taste for landscape gardening
Had been of some use to his sons since Eden
In laying out the parterres for a people
Along (the former) mudslopes of a world
Whence they may gather nosegays.   I recall
That e'en the Heavenly Garden set on heights
Is laid out, measured oft, by One—a man—
You'd call him "a Surveyor."   He's called
    Christ
Up there where value finds its estimate.
And mark, this old word *Value* means *Valeur*,
A fighting quality.   Red to the rim
Of his great life stood Christ, with battle
    splashed,
As he hewed his way through.   He now "sur-
    veys"
The wall-environment around His park
(Or camp).   "It is the measure of a man!"
He cries.   Of what man think you? of Himself?
Of any man who's wall around a people.

"George the Surveyor." Yes, the term will
    hold.

The Blue Ridge mountains with their dip and
    dare   .
Stretched their cerulean curve and climb o'er
    thee ;
What thoughts and projects, Washington, arose
To that grand forehead's democratic crown
(The only crown for which 'tis worth to sweat)
The Dare to free a people didst thou dream?
The Pause to bend and wait till the great
    hour?
Be resolute, be noble thou, O soul !
Canst thou fortell when some great hour shall
    call
Its summons to great deeds across the soil
Where vacant now thy days slip by, the sun
A scorching eyeball in the heavens to blind.
Strike deeper in the arid wastes thy roots,

O soul! whose pulse springs Palm-like to the
    Blue,
And wait — till the great God-thrill through
    thee run,
Creative.

       Thou art destined for the Dare.
The touch that wakens thee to azure air
Sweeps o'er thy branches with the living Breath
That fructifies to quench the thirst of men
As through the tawny desert's death-mist dread,
They urge their flagging way — lo! their wild
    cry —
The undulant blue shadows lace the Vague,
The enchanted murmur of the Morning Calm
Breaks, like the illumined chorus after death —
They see thy date-palm's Crown soar o'er her
    streams!

Thy thought leaps high as God's great sentinels,

Those lips, O Washington, would match great
    Mars',
Thy forehead answers to thine eye to-night,
It flames and searches the perspective's gloom,
Thine eyes, O Washington, that see the streak,
The silver dawn-streak light that grows and
    domes
Into the soaring of the Blue, the arch
Above that throne,—the land where every man
Sits crowned because he's man. Yea, doughty
    men
(The dynasties Columbia counts and counts
Upon her rosary of stellar might)
Out-rank the dynasties of fibril kings.

Alone on thee, George the Surveyor, hang
The hopes of a whole people in this hour.
And yet thou standest silent and aloof.
The brook that chatters spends itself in froth.
From out the awful hush where Ocean thinks,

Depth upon depth in folded silence dread,
Ascend the giant words that plunge and hurl
Their battle-cry around a blanching world.

Still the reproach grows: "He's so silent!
    look!"
The statue stands, a silence. Cold, you say?
It's thought. The fire-heats in artist-soul,
And white heats in the marble's snowy breast
In fusion met. Passion divine! and Thought
Was born—this Thought that stabs you sud-
    denly.
What fires wed in thy great soul to-night,
Thou silent man? What Thought discloses now
In thee, Columbia's Cæsar, its august?
Alone on thee, O Washington, this hour
The hopes of a whole people hang. On thee
Who'rt left to-night with just two thousand
    men,
And gallant sheaf of generals who stand firm.

The life of the United States dies low,
A flickering flame. No flag e'en have these
    troops
To bear before them in great war. And strong,
Sting the proud words from out the Parliament
Where England sits in storied might of men,
The varied lights of statesmanship, like panes
Of annal'd glass down her great Minster's
    aisles.
Their hands yet hold the leash that's bit in
    mouths
Of a tempestuous tribe out there, "the States,
We'll rein in soon and feed with tea-leaves."
    Lion,
Whose ocean-roar is heard around a world,
Three words of thine thunder through Parlia-
    ment :
"Can Britain fail?" The man who walks alone
Beyond the edge of bayonet-gleam out there,
Beside the edge of icy corpse of stream,

With no proud banner shaking out its light
Of promise for the morrow, bites the words
Between his teeth.   I would beware of lips
Like those, O Britain, for they're very dread.
And then, that Eye, that's long accustomed
To unimpeded horizons, sees—what?
Columbia fail?   She who may belt her path
With dew-light glory and with scarlet dusk?
Columbia fail?   She who from east to west
May sweep her gaze that fronts the eternal foam
Of seas which rock in thunderous murmurings
Around a world?   Ocean will bate its breath,
And lay its golden flecks of foam, its coins,
At feet of Her who studs one golden word
Upon her brow for nations : **Liberty.**
Columbia fail?

        Yes, but the night dies down,
And fold on fold its awful wing creeps on.
No hope to lift its glory, sheen on sheen,

Looms as the land to homesick eye's return

Across the sunset wave, and strong tears roll

Down stalwart faces that have faced the bleak;

No flag to flame its force, its beckoning,

Looms in its grandeur, o'er our gaze to-night.

Art Thou not there? The stellar dust that
   whirls

In pathless space, from Thy lit chariot-wheels

It sprays, each drop a world that breaks to
   height

Of being, held by Thee whose Hand is rein

O'er the blue vault of the sun-systems' swirl

Lo, as Thou movest on the Infinite,

Watchman of Israel, who slumberest not.

Art Thou not there? Dost Thou not send Thy
   word

Thy plunging meteor-word to say to earth

"'Tis God the Timeless, to thy knees to-
   night,

·Worship the Might that can deliver man."

The cannon's roar shudders across the night
From distant darken'd heights of Morristown.
Its eye of flame rips shadows.   Through its
    glare
Dead eyeballs stare upon a vacant sky,
While gurgling down the Dark, prophetic voice
Of heroes' blood speaks to the greater Vast:

Stand forth, O God Almighty, in this night!
Our cause is just, give us a sign, 'tis just!
Look how the nations gather 'neath the beck
Of each dread finger looming as their hosts
March on beneath its shadowed garment's power,
"Our lighthouse," shout their voices in the van.
Yet, Orient's crescent waxes to no moon.
England's proud standard shows the lion fierce
To fall upon his prey; the claws distend.
Beneath her standard crawl three abject men
And cling.   They sign their names while na-
    tions laugh:

The Turk, who whets his promising scimetar
Upon the long, bleached bones of steadfast men
Who held thy faith, O Britain, the same faith
That says "I'm Christ's," as lo! the gold cross
    looms
Above thy crown's height where a ruby rocks
And restless tells of great blood spilt in vain.
The Turk, who's sponsor for his scimetar;
The Egyptian gentleman, whose haul (in sport)
How many concubines to stock his harem?
Whose haul (in sport) how much of thy gold-
    drops
O Britain, wrung from sweat of thy earth's
    sons?
Yet, 'tis the Egyptian gentleman. Be fair,
Fair with fine manners, Britain, and protect.
Take care of the Sick Man, the Yellow'd Shah—
Upon thy insular pivot, Britain, turn
And watch the dupes to whom thy guns dic-
    tate.

Stand forth, O Judge of nations, in this night,
Our cause is just, give us a sign, 'tis just !
The sweep of Slavic bird moves o'er lone snows
That shroud the cautious on-come of the Bear;
The "*Gott mit uns*" stares with white eye-
      balls dread
Upon the standard whose background is black
With belchings of hot war, a spectre-gaze;
The throes of nations streak upon their flags
The earthquake-mutterings under which they
      fall ;
Imperial ermine's spotted with black flecks
That ooze upon the bland of regal gaze ;
The scorpion crawls on immemorial walls
Of China hoar, standard to sting her hosts;
Through Vale of Roses where the nightingale
Pours to the night his love-rill lit with moon,
That moon whose tears are pearls dropped down
      the Gulf
As slow o'er its lit billowing she moves

THE SCARLET-VEINED.

Seeking her love the Sun—her soul, herself
Libation to his light; across this Eden
Passes that flag whose rude primeval roar
Blanches the blush of rose—the Lion stalks,
And woman's hopes sink with each sinking sun.

The land whose soil was fed from Marathon,
Whose Thought hath opened paths to deathless
    June,
Pink dawn along the old, gnarled, branching
    years,
The makers of new Meadows mad with morn
Where men yet bend and drink of mazy springs,
In epic draughts or lyric wine or cruse
Filled by a golden hand, the Academe's,
At doors of immortality ; the Land
Whence sway of Gods still dictates to a world
In vocal silences where Art divine
Rules from the brow of Zeus or lips of Love—
This Land, the jewel of Ægean spray,

THE SCARLET-VEINED.

Who wore an Orient as a victor-star,
Great Hellas! once again thou standest forth
The champion of the Idea; and this, the Thought
That grooved itself in Letters of thine art
First, in the kingly signature of Christ
Titled on shuddering conquest of His Cross.

Thou, gazing through the sightless eyeballs,
    wreck
Of crumbled empires, Britain's Orient toy,
The shattered golden Crescent that erewhile
As moon of Mahomet re-lit the brows
Of Egypt's marble gods, pale with great Past;
Nightly with silver mellowings, bent rapt
Above the voice of immemorial stream—
Isis divine the lotus-breast Ideal;
And, as the glittering arc, electric span
Binding barbaric Asia to the West,
Flashed will of Sultan down its scimetar
(That mirrored deep England's acute consent);

Thou, gazing o'er God's whitening moon-re-
    vealed,
The Ottoman's ghastly distance of decay—
Shalt lift thy standard of the God of gods,
Veined from the empyrean, on that height
Where once great Pallas war-wreathed stood,
    her eyes
A threat, blue lights of war that menaced worlds.

The Kalpas', ages seven, the ages vast
That climb on India's standard, what say they
To this age battering at her effete doors
For entrance?

                God, Ancient of days, the Now,
Veil of the All, the Timeless in all Time,
Before Whose glance the ages flit like globes
Of iridescent foam a-down the roar
Of cataracts that kneel 'neath mountain's Eye;
Thou, Alpha and Omega of Thy worlds

The stars are stairways only, vestibule
Unto Thy Vast, Ancient of mysteries.
The constellations' epic Chronicles
Tell but the rim unto Thy radiance ;
They, golden portals of untravelled shrine,
The belfry trembling with the Voice whose peal
Upbuilds the dazzled dome-reach of those suns
That countless crowd, and carve one Orient
    ai le
Whirli.'g its incense-cloud up, up, still up—
The vaporous silver of adoring worlds
At foot of the great Altar's golden—GOD.

Stand forth, O God of armies, iu this night !
Thou hast a standard to lead ou to light,
That standard is the star-hosts' broidered gleam.
Across each night it streams in fiery mist
Held in the hand of cohorts infinite,
Whose grip upon the staff untightens ne'er,
Whose thirst in this dread march alone is slaked

At source of Thy soul's wine. Thunder their
  voice,
Their finger's lightning indicates the goal
Towards which Thou movest, Mightiest, the goal
Of Armageddon where Thy judgments fall.
Stand forth, O God of cohorts, in this night,
Our cause is just, give us a sign, 'tis just !
Is there not sign along Thy Heavens to help?

Lo! in that night's renown when Pharaoh's
  hosts
Encamped beside Red waters, vast on vast,
Perspective dread of war-bred chariots,
Warriors whose way mowed down old worlds,
  and wrote
New hieroglyphs of blood on Chaldea's dust,
A Cartouche kingly ; lo! in that dread day
When Pharaoh's serried spears held the great
  glance
Of his great gazing sun-god Amen-Ra,

A sparkle that sent shouts above the Blue—
The obelisk of God, His pillar'd cloud,
Yea, God Himself, moved through the awful
    hush
That fell, as slow the night of Egypt welled;
Nay, God it was who trod down suns,
And blotted out the bloom of Nile's great shores,
Pressing upon the River 'till it fled
An ooze of darkness dread, an Ethiop' streak
From cataracts to sea. Still welled that Dark,
Stealing along the knots of dazzled spears,
Blackening the guard and rear-guard of the
    king—
Pharaoh! thy horses' crests are darkening!
Help! for the Pharaoh, help! his phalanx-veins
Date from the throes of gods, e'er Egypt was,
They're red with the veined raiment of great
    Ra !
They're black from one dread touch, O king
    of kings,

Pharaoh, thy horse's crests are darkening,

Like those gaunt plumes which wave on fun-
eral car,

The dead goes by!

                    The living God goes by

And drowns in dusk the power that crumbled

thrones.

Stand forth, O Watchman dread, in this our
night!

Rip from Thy heavens star-veins of galaxies

That roll in restless waiting round Thy throne.

To pulse forever as our onward lamp.

For pilot as for ploughman, sea or land,

Lo! is Thy hand not ready to indite

A message new writ from Thine azure Vast,

A message new leaping in scarlet veins,

Pinn'd with thine own star-promises? the
chords

THE SCARLET-VEINED.

Like strings upon an instrument profound
Whence floats a music whose one theme
In endless harmony of blended voice
Sings to a world the symphony—𝕷𝖎𝖇𝖊𝖗𝖙𝖞.

A silence awful holds the land. A pause.
The creak stupendous of the earth was felt
As slow with awful words of prophecy,
She rocks from red to red, from sunset's path
To dawn-aisles where the Face of God is sun.
Darkness upon our forces. Midnight black,
A hand of Dark whose fangs are smeared with
    death.
Is there no hope, Eternal, Who once mad'st
The wrath of man to praise Thee?

Through the great Dark whose clutch steals
    close, a voice—
The guns of England streak their flame-wrath
    red

In bands upon the sky. Britain! thy wrath
The Lord Almighty takes for His own plan
And belts a Standard on the thunder-cloud
Through which the eyes celestial crowd and
　　crowd,
Star-nebulæ of worlds, of forming worlds to
　　be—
For, out this stellar mist that wreathes the
　　night,
States, peoples, powers arise like fountain-foam
That springs perennial from the earth's dark
　　breast,
Renews itself in sparkle, globe on globe,
An atom measuring Immensity.
The Flag for nations! Lo, Britain's gun-streaks
　　red
Toss their renown upon God's platform, Night;
Promethean breath of Britain rolls white mist
As belts upon the forming banner, Liberty !
And God's own hand tears constellations up,

And pins their promises upon this Blue.
Nations shall look to It. Their fading eyes
Gather new gleams of hope. The hour has
  rung.
Star-veins that part the sea, shout Harborage !
And their united voices' spheric tones
Still leap in lyric chant as once they sang
In their great orbits' fire : **In God we Trust.**

The man to lead in vanguard of great men
Stands up.   His gaze is awful down this night's
Great eagle-wing of overshadowing.
Stand. still, ye nations, for the hour has rung.
There is a Standard. God's Might and one Man
Who hurls his heroes o'er the Delaware.

*　　*　　*　　*　　*

June 14, 1777.

The shadow vast of death that clutched the
  shores

THE SCARLET-VEINED.

Of the long river's answering pallid face
Has passed away. Down in the trenches'
    depths
One stood, and grappled with a Form
Dismounted, hideous, whose laugh played loose
Among the dead, whose breath blew orchestra
Across the fleshless hands that streaked the air.
They closed in vital grapple, the great Two—
Thou Washington, with those fore-ordained lips,
And thou gaunt Shadow, moving awfully.
The great result stands pillar'd on all Time.
The man who dares face shadows, merits sun.
You'll see him in a moment where he stands
And does a deed that's fraught with conse-
    quence
In this fair city, Philadelphia call'd.

Two rivers, yea of life, encircle her.
The belt of land that's stretched from gleam
    to gleam,

Forms, in its streets, the chords upon a lute
Whence martial music floated, in the ring
Of great men's steps this good year 'Seventy-
    Seven.
The quaint old city's birth dates from afar.
The feet of Hudson, Stuyvesant, De Vries
Smoothed out the savage furrows, partially.
And then thou cam'st, serene and sun-lit face,
With thy great project for this belt of land
To found a commonwealth, self-governing,
Whose roots draw sap from the great principles
Of fundamental faith ; whose branches wave
Free as God's air to spread where'er they list.
Still hold the quaint old city's forest streets
Her forest names, in echoes sylvan, sweet,
Of the far Time where God invited first
His birds to sing upon the sunlit air
The outward music of the tree's great heart.

The quaint old city's name dates from afar,

Penn named it Philadelphia. Its great root
Once grappled deep on shores of the Levant
To whom God's message to His churches
    came,—
The Seven (you'll find them writ within the
    Book),
Among them, Philadelphia, the name means
The *love of brotherhood.* Well-named, great
    man,
Whose policy towards the savage—Peace!
Two words stand out on thine escutcheon proud:
Mercy and Justice, the initial steps
By which thou mounted'st to the Indian's
    heart.
· The highest throne in all God's measurements:
Steadfast dominion o'er the hearts of men.

The quaint old Quaker city on the streams
Inherits still mild faces (that yet know
Good cheer. Their taste's a relic, Anglican).

Its sleepy, dreamy, say you? Not the speed
Of great New York, or brain - spin of the
    "Hub."
Most surely, Philadelphia's not New York
Where, with a headlong rush, we hurl our-
    selves
Against—His smile that says, "Go back, my
    child,
Begin again more quietly. It took
How many æons to enrich the mud
Whereon the city of Manhattan rests?"
Nor Boston, that spins round upon her hub,
And sometimes stands stock still and loses
    time
Through gaze at her domed forehead in the
    Bay.
There have been peacocks who lost wondrous
    chance
Of succulent sweet crumbs spread for their fare
By spreading to the fair their Vanity,

And standing vaster than King Solomon
Before a travell'd lady, Sheba call'd—
While homely little squirrels gobbled All.

Most surely Philadelphia's not New York :
But Gothic is not Greek, nor Byzantine,
Nor yet the old Gigantic whence they drew
Their nutriment,—the temples on the Nile.
Enjoy the Egyptian, Karnak's awful might,
The work of men who worshipped. And the
    Greek
The work of men who thought. And down
    to-day
The Gothic, work of men who dreamed. Be-
    ware
Of climbing up into God's Judgment-seat.
You could not, surely, see as far as He,
E'en if you climbed.

              Along the stream of Time

Leapt God's great word of message to that
    town
Of Philadelphia, yea, from Him who held
The seven stars—His churches, in His hand.
He that hath ears let *him* hear what God says
In His great message now, in this good year
Of 'Seventy-seven. A word writ with a pen
Dipp'd in His sunrise-veins, His moon's path
    hoar,
His cauldron of the stars where worlds swim up.

You see that sunny cloud along the Blue?
Follow its pointing finger as it floats
Still on. It stays to-day and wreaths itself
Above a Tower, from whose quaint galleries'
    height   .
The vistas wind through many murky ways
Of this complex existence—MAN, and find
The one strong civic citadel within,
Surrendering never to the shocks of chance,

Building above, howe'er down-crushed, subdued,
Finding its way still up through clods or kings,
The one supreme in all my manhood's urge—
The Love of Freedom—**Independence** call'd.

In Independence Hall one year agone,
One year before this good date 'Seventy-seven,
A future hung upon a breathless pause,
As, slow, a massive parchment was unrolled,
And great men's eyes glittered across its blank.
Shall we throw down, with iron hand, the
    glove,
The gauntlet of our signature? Around
Belts Britain her stupendous — men who're
    carved
In tactics of bright steel, flanked with the
    shell
That tore its way to conquest in two spheres.
They tilted, yea, at Time, those warriors,
Time the great shadow of the Infinite

That e'er unrolls its boundless azure line,
The sky-line of the Ever-New, the View
Expanding in soul-ardor's light to heights.
Time whose recording hand is held in God's,
Held the great pen above the parchment's
    blank.
Think you the dim papyrus-groves on Nile
Whispered in ages gone momentous words
The generations were to carve for e'er
Upon their page, from Mena to the Man
The Word, through Whom the furrowed ages'
    thought
Voiced its supreme, the Λόγος, Christ?

                              The New
That's still the Old, recorded its great birth,
In eastward room of Independence Hall.
Name after name sowed its immortal, wrote
Its shining track upon that bleak—the Un-
    known.

But they knew. They felt (in signing that
    great Roll
The Magna Charta of our liberties),
Those prophets stern, the very pulse of God
Who holds the hand of Time upon that lock
That opens a new doorway up the day.

To-day, to-day this good year 'Seventy-seven,
A doorway open stands in Independence Hall.
Wait at the threshhold with bowed, reverent
    head,
I counsel it, before this Council in the room.
Your eye sweeps round the circle brave of men
Who've stood the strain of being quite sincere—
America's young Congress. Nay, they're old
These men in knowledge of tradition, law
The Lord laid down; His first-born : Light,
    that's free.
They gravely wait upon a central word.
The table's strewn with quite a curious mesh

Of colored light. Is it prismatic gleam
From storied windows shredding their great
   rays?
Nay, but the panes are plain white glass
Like windows in the poor man's simple hut,
White as the mountain-breath of smoke that
   curls
From cabin of the pioneer afar.
No accessory frames these faces strong,
These carvers of our Life. From out their lives
Will sweep the mighty aisles where men may
   kneel
And worship God who steadied them in storm.

Yes, but this mesh of colors? rainbow-gleam
From somewhere, somehow, saying "Night is
   past,
Shout your great shout, the Lord's a man of war
And has led on? Your Miriam-timbrel clash?
In one great moment, pivotal, you'll hear

"They fought from heaven, the very star-veins
    fought."
Wait the result.

The tints that tinge this board
Are the old flags of the old colonies :
Connecticut's, her motto stamped in gilt ;
Putnam's,—well-done thou grand old Puritan,
With thy "Appeal to Heaven" in brave relief !
Thy "Trust in God ! (but keep your powder
    dry)";
Moultrie's blue flag, a crescent in the bend ;
Virginia's Yellow, with its menace-coil,
Its serpent legend "Do not tread on me !"
And Massachusetts' with its Evergreen,
Its Pine unfading on whose bark is cut
For Unbelief to scan, just "Old Put's" words.
(The present proves that they have quite
    avail'd).
Dare to rely on Heaven when all is dark,

Her stars will laurel thee with aureate light.

The Light, the first-born Light, streams through
    the panes,
And focuses its flash upon a Web
Of iridescent sheen—a dew-light belt,
A scarlet dusk, paths that stretch east, stretch
    west—
Repeated o'er and o'er. And silver flecks
Of foam are they? from out the Ocean-war
Of elements? Nay, look! look closer yet,
And see the stars roll their perennial fires
Upon this standard.

              Once again there's hush
In the old Hall. The eyes of Congress turn .
Towards a Man who sits in their great midst ;
For on his word a beetling moment waits.

As when, along the crags and storied cliffs
That hold the history of the Ocean's face

THE SCARLET-VEINED.

In seam and scar—the fastnesses of Thought,
One spur lifts up beyond the cliff-path's streak,
And holds the sudden smite of the great sun,
And echoes back the shout of salt-wind's voice—
Spray'd with Immensity, kin to God's sky,
The eagle mount amongst the crested crags;
Arises in the midst of granite men
One Man.

      In vanguard of great men he towers,
A silhouette against an old world's quake.
You see him : Washington. Three syllables
That wrote a new word in the book of life,
It spells the All that makes life any worth—
Home, Country, Liberty.

        With onward look
That eyes of genius own, his gaze commands
A future. For to-day, in this good place,
A standard must be chosen for a people.
Slowly, as when before the prophet's eye
Trained in aloneness, silence, to arrive

At God's great ventures, yea, in Bethlehem
The little town that bourgeons like the soul
Apex of all creation's symmetry—
The sons of Jesse passed, and the Voice said
"This is not My anointed;" the great hand
Of Washington puts by the flags and flags
Which Congress lifts to meet his onward gaze.
The iron hand of the great warrior
Grasps one great fold.   It is the Word
Writ to the City Philadelphia by the Pen
Dipped in the sunrise-veins, the moon's path
    hoar,
God's cauldron of the stars where worlds swim
    up—
The message to the land that He elects.

The iron hand of the great warrior,
The lordlier hand of the great man
Tarries.   On him who marched breast-high in
    blood

And hew'd our way right through, decision
    hangs.
I hear the heart-throb of a wheeling world,
I hear the greater heart-throb of great men.

        *   *   *   *   *

Above, in the gray Tower a gray-haired man,
A patriot sits. His hand is on the cords
That hold the Bell, the great Bell—𝕷𝖎𝖇𝖊𝖗𝖙𝖞.
It thundered out, one year agone, the Word
That spoke around two waiting hemispheres,
As name by name went down, in tossing
    shouts,
Upon the Page that severed us for aye
Unto ourselves.
                The old man's face recalls
That day: millennial moment on Time's clock.

A spot of fire like spurt from a star-wheel
Burns on his cheek just now, this patriot old.

Closer he grasps the cords. And, solemn, waits
Like dawn's gray face that feels the advance
   of fire.

A voice leaps bound on bound the Tower's
   stairs :
"Ring, Ring, they've chosen. Washington
   has said.
Ring, Ring, we have a Standard from the
   stars—"
The old bell rocks and sways against the
   walls,
The pulse of patriots pours its leaping fire
In clash of iron voices : Ring, O Bell,
Ring, Ring, Ring out the vast horizon's light—
Thou rock'st men's chains on lone Siberia's
   snows
With utterance prophetic. Through the rose
That blooms upon the breast of woman, bound,
A hope thrills up, of sacred home and child.

Across the heats of Asia, crawls the snake,
The scorpion, within its walls. Thou Bell
Doom'st it to die, thou ring'st an era new.
Dash great- desire and dare in hearts of men,
Bind in one common weal, one commonwealth,
The rich who reaps, the poor who sows the
    seed.
Enfranchise man where'er he groans and waits.
Ring, drop on drop, the rounded verity :
One blood unites the ploughman and the prince
Yea, as one scarlet fire threads through the
    spheres.
Ring, Ring O Bell, the Flag's full fluttering
    voice—
(From night 'twas born, the night was needful,
    see,
For mellowing of a star-purpose vast),
Ring out O Bell, its tidings down the tides
That mount in sapphire glory foamed with
    stars :—

Fear ye no night, O ye United States,
Each dusk is witness on great Heaven's dome
Ye'll stand. The stars nail it along the night.
Fear ye no night, O ye United States,
The night of party jealousies, of strife,
Where factions war, and thunders roll their car,
Where the live tongues leap from the light-
    ning's mail,
And the vast Void is vocal round your sail—
Your prow, your Scarlet-Veined ploughs up
    the stars,
Those harbor-lights of God's great Common-
    wealth,
The bubbling lights for nations round your
    Barque.

To
his Majesty

GEORGE THE FIRST

KING OF HELLAS

The Inheritor of her giant Past
The Herald of her garlanded To-morrow.

Προφητεία

The Morning Star above the scythèd moon
  Crowns the great dawning's brink,
Hellas! thy stellar Past upon thy brow,
Re-throned through throes of night upon the
    Now,
  Dost watch the Crescent sink!

VOICES.

From Hellas—For Hellas.

ONCE more thine ancient fires burn, Hel-
lenic might,
On Athos' height,
And face, with lurid forehead o'er the blue
expanse,
The Orient's lance.
On Cretan Ida's fountained peak the watch-
man waits.
Ægean's gates,
The portals of thy crimson-hearted heroes, ope
In sunrise-hope.
Forward! With memories red of Marathon's
great gaze
Through Asian maze,
Face Britain's vaunted brawn, great Europe's
treachery,
Thews of Thermopylæ!

VOICES.

Voices from Hellas.

THEIR shout went up to the Sun
      Ages gone,
To the white brows, recording, of gods,
When Herodotus read of The Fight
That fashioned those Hellenes a might
    In the teeth of a fulgurous dawn,

The Orient buttressed on brawn
      Ages gone,
Pale like the peopled haze of hell,
A whirlwind, edged, o'er the shuddering main
It swept, it clashed. It shall meet again
    Little Hellas buttressed on brain.

Her shout goes up to the sun
      In this dawn,

To the heart of the great God of gods.

Alone midst Europe's craven gun-light,

Alone to lift the Christ-flag aright,

Veined with the ancient ichor of might—

    Little Hellas buttressed on right!

From Mount Olympus.

,

ONCE more ye whirl your glance a-down
    that height,
The fount of the idea—of gods for man.
See ! through the valley's serpentining light,
Dread mirror of the hornèd moon, the wan
Thin daylight looks.   Fuller and faster still
The Orient pours.   Her hordes' vermilion
    Hope,
Fire-sheeted from great Tophet's fanned anvil,
Roars a red rain.   The devil's gate is ope.
Nay, whirl our shout round the great stars, we
    men,
The beaked hearts of great Hellas hold the hour.
No more as once the war midst gods again
Contending, calls.   The one who blends their
    power

VOICES.

Into one cause of man for man stands out—
Christ with the human eyes has led the shout!

Mors Janua Vitae.

STAND, O ye Hellenes, stand!
"Three Hundred" against All;
Stand in the rocky clefts of your will,
The thin red line of great Hellas still,
Stand!

Stand, O ye Hellenes, stand!
Your thirty centuries
Are glowing before ye, and ray ye all o'er
If ye'll smite as never and never before—
Stand!

Stand, O ye Hellenes, stand!
Of fiery transport born,
Grapple onward with knee, with fist, with teeth,
Wrench out from disaster immortal wreath—
Stand!

Cœur De Lion 1189.
The Lion=Hearted 1897.

O H, for one steel-strong Presence at thy
prow,

England, finessing while Christ's flag goes down!

Where is thy vaunted *cœur de Lion* now

To answer with its roar the Orient's frown?

Plantagenets thou countest, royal roll

Buzzing o'er Turkish sweetmeats wrapt in pelf;

PLANTAGENET is not: Great scarlet soul,

Who for thy Thorn-Crowned flung away himself.

To-day thy *cœur de Lion* crouches, pale

From prowl of Bear and scream of Teuton bird;

Arise, dead Cid!* our manhood's hoarse "All
hail!"

* The reader will recall how the prayers of the faithful and
the tooth of St. Apollonia having failed, they set the dead Cid
from his tomb in Burgos at the head of the host, and routed the
red Orient.

73

Awaits thine awful face, thy silent word.

Arise, thou gaunt but gauntleted red Might,

And hurl thine England on the Orient's fight!

The Slavic Bird.

ABOVE those ancient hill-tops, where the
dove
Panted its message bright of irised rain,
A vulture-cloud wheels darkening, above
The solemn Vast—the unmeasured mounds
of slain.
Armenia! arching o'er thy crimsoned lands
Two dread wings stretch ; steady they wait,
their sweep
That Standard's double eye whose move com-
mands
From Stamboul's silent chess-play to the leap
Of the Pacific sea. Is it to help,
Thou Russian might? to succor, save? and led
By thee the nations learn? for thy dread
self

Thy Standard's dark advancement o'er the
dead?

Is this thy power? lo! thy huge wings un-
roll.

A nation's bulk consists in her great soul!

ffor Crete and Armenia.

FORWARD, ye nations, in the name of
Heaven !
The Cross that wrapped your hosts in fiery
swathe,
Saint George's gleam, thou England to thee
given
Down thine illumined Past, to-day 'twill bathe
Thy unsheathed steel. Leap from your bond-
aged sheath,
Ye swords of Albion, to avenge the hands
Stretched in a white appeal to ye, where death
Streaks the gaunt air in Islam's defamed lands.
We men, whose flag claims Heaven's great star-
ship dread
For pilot, in our veins rocks the red blood
Of brotherhood with Britain's life, faith-fed.

VOICES.

Is it not forward in the name of God?
ONE took the greater risk upon a Cross
And saved a world in Calvary's red loss!

Voices.

WHAT voices swing with the wild bird's
    wing
  Fluttering on Stamboul's shore,
Sweeping along the red twilight's trail,
  Calling, and o'er and o'er
Flinging on Mosque and Seraglio's domes
  Their utmost plaint at the door?

On the Dardanelles' breast in infamous rest
  The guns of England lie,
A holiday Red at the halliard's head,
  The Cross of Christ on high!
Idly a breath curls the crimsoning wave:
  The *ennui* of Britain's sigh.

Like a giant wound, without cry or sound,

VOICES.

The red sun falls and falls,
An awful drop on the dead, dumb day,
    A requiem that calls
To every drop of red manhood's blood
    In that fleet at the Sultan's walls.

It utters to-day and to-morrow's to-day
    The Orient's crimson shame;
The Orient's shame, did I rashly cry?
    'Tis Christians' scarlet shame
That hears the wild surge of its brethren's blood—
    And plays the diplomatists' game!

And idly floats like the painted boats
    That children set adrift,
While the blood sobs on with each falling sun;—
    No hand leaps forth to lift
From the soddened woe. But, ye nations, hark!
For this red sun moves up the Orient-dark
    And speaks to Him who will sift!

On History's Wall.

S O fallen, so lost,
      England to-day!
Thy guns plough the moonlight
At Crete with their noonlight:
      Lit infamy's ray.

So fallen, so lost,
      England in might!
Thy faith? in the Prophet
Whose sons dip in Tophet
      Their hands of red light.

So fallen, so vain,
      England, thy vaunt!
Thy Christ shudders, dying,

VOICES.

Thy colors a-flying
>   At Crete toss their taunt.

So fallen, so shrunk,
>   Britain *"sans bornes"!*
In Turkish bonds grappled,
Thy conscience? a dappled,
>   Dead-gold, a God's scorn.

For the hand, trembling, stretched
>   (Thou, Britain, know well)
On Crete's Calvary, writes
From its crimson's dread heights
>   Thy Mene Tekel.

PATRIOTIC POEMS.

The Flag in the Dardanelles.

OF all the wonders that the Old World
    shows,
Of storied heights, Imperial gloom or gleam,
One sight stupendous, growth of a grand dream,
Lifts in the crimson haze of Orient-beam,
    The Flag of Washington leads empires on.

Fortressed upon his crimes the Sultan sits,
A smile triumphant bridges the blue straits,
Where, impotent, the might of nations waits.
The smile Sultanic its red scheeming sates?
    Not while the Scarlet-Veined leads empires
    on.

Unfurled to thunderous haze of Moslem might,
O Flag of Washington, in this great hour,

A challenge, thou, in teeth of storied power;
No lust of empire tempts thee, golden dower—
   The cause of Man is thine, O Flag, sail on!

On! where the "Powers" are powerless to pass,
In van of empires thou the guiding rod,
On! for the cause of Man is cause of God!
God swept His stars one morn thy face upon—
   The cause of God is thine, O Flag, sail on!

Nature's Vote.

GOD'S great big golden Dollar rises daily
   on the dawning,
  And scatters golden plenty to Uncle Sam's
    vast fold,
Tell me why this fuss on voting? God's poli-
    tics are chosen !
  The darkness claims the silver, the moon
    that's fed from gold.

In Memoriam Maceo.

"He being dead, yet speaketh."

AT Punta Brava hast thou fallen to-day,
Leading thy Star through the red car-
nage-haze?
Upon Spain's lip a Judas-smile finds way,
Broadening to laughter and to triumph-lays?
From Punta Brava shall thy star ascend,
O Cuban patriot, thy standard's star
That with great Freedom's galaxy must blend
And burn before the dark of nations far.
Shall the Castilian smile from camp to king?
Not while on *Brava* soil there lives a
soul,
Not while the alchemy of Freedom's ring,
Married to man, gleams toward one golden
goal.

Thy meteor-purpose, Maceo, shall burn
Upon thy comrades' souls, the battle turn!

To Grover Cleveland.

Chief Executive.

O THOU who waitest at the helm this hour,
    Thou whom Columbia honored with her
    trust,
To voice her will, to represent her power,
    Why on thy pen Executive this rust
When the great cry of man for Liberty
    Obliges thy great torch to light his land?
O shaker of the Lion and the sea,
    Thou who didst fetter Anarchy's red hand,
Thou from the Putnam battle-blood that
    knew
    Nor danger, nor dishonor, nor delay
When the fair Right lifteth her face to sue
    For manhood's instant arm, cost what it
    may—

Carve out, with Pen, a path for Cuba free,
Oh, seize to-day thine opportunity !

England's Pet Bird.

IN the Zoo of the nations a marvellous sight
  On the sands of Time appears,
Madam Europe stands up with her lorgnette
    deep,
  At the crested vision leers.

A trainer of animals great and small
  Struts forth in the garish light,
His crow rhyming on with the death-clock's
    tick—
  And fair Europe's cheek turns white.

He faces the bear with the grizzled hair,
  Four hundred years older than he,
Quite ancient enough this bird to instruct—
  The Turkey instructs Brother B. !

He eyes the two-headed Kaiser-bird,
  With his one old-sinner head;
The Eagles of Rome that o'er Asia screamed,
  Coquet, then shiver—they've fled!

But marvel of marvels, the biped that once
  Caressed him (caged in the South),
Look! To-day he has got a hitching-strap
  In the English donkey's mouth.

The Prize=Winner.

I HAD a large prize for the Zoo,
  For the denizens of the den,
I slowly strolled through the garden's fold,
  And, quite anxiously, scanned each pen :

There was the British lion
  With a bluster in every blare !
Yet he feared to fight for the Hellenes' right,
  Can't he bear The Prize to his lair ?

Our Eagle was posing well
  For a new dollar-greenback die,
Yet no quill from his wing has writ the Grand
    Thing
  To sustain *Cuba Libre* as I.

The monkey was mincing the airs

Of a *Dreibund* member, quite pale,
Sniffling well to the organ was plaintive Jack
    Morgan,
  Quite Red, White and Green to his tail.

I heard two big buzzards talking:
  " *Mille pardons!* " * * " *Entschuldigen Sie!* "
On the walls that were Alsace, a good deal of
    tall "sass,"
  An Eagle (or eager) war-glee.

Just look at that grandiose Bird!
  He sweeps from the lands of the Pole,
But his glance it is double, 'twill give nations
    trouble
  From Scotia to Corea's *rôle.*

The sick Turkish paroquet
  On the Sultan-odalisque's arm
Is really quite well: the "Powers" are pell-mell!

That red on his wing is Blood, warm!

They all really deserve my prize;
   To whom shall I give it, you think?
But I've made up my mind, and I'm quite far
      from blind,
   You can guess. One guess in a wink!

There he comes, the Prize-Winner, sure!
   A wailer, spelt W-e-y-l-e-r, you say?
My Booby Prize-Winner without triumph's din-
      ner:
   The real SPANISH DONKEY to-day.

Expectations.

"WHOM do you pray for, darling, to-
night?"
Mamma said to the curly toss
Of childhood's ringlets upon her knee.
The arch little face looked up with glee:
"For McKinley and Santa Klaus!"

The Loftiest Word.

FROM the magnet-touch of the great To-day
    That tosses them up to their starry way
The flags are writing along the sky
In the quivering Red and White and Blue
    (The Liberty-ink that nations sue)
The loftiest word in the circling hum
Of Life—that volume of smile and sigh :
    AMERICANUS SUM !

July 4th.

POEMS OF NATURE.

The Skylark.

U P!

Through the dew-light when Dawn holds her cup
To the rim of the scarlet sun,
O'er the sparkles that float and run
To a zenith whose breath's begun—
Up!

Up!
With thy beak in that Deep, in a wine
Whose brim is a blooming divine,
Upwelling for this thirst of thine
To mount the blue Infinite line—
Up!

Up!
O'er the woodlands that fill their green cup
With the gurgle of birds and streams,
With the sunlight in tangled beams,
The forest's dawn-echo of dreams—
Up!

Up!
The thunderous octaves of ocean,
The Infinite's epic to man,
Grow lessening and less. The blue span
A vaporous streak, thinning—wan—
Up!

Up!
The shimmer of silver worlds, star flight,
Falls a cloud wreath on azure light,
Up! thy wild wing aspires the height,
What margins of mystery in sight?
Up!

Up !

And thy shower of song in the cup

Which to mortal lips is given

For a moment of unveiled heaven—

The cry of an utmost Eden !

Up !

In the Orchard.

FULL-DRESS the apple-tree ladies,
  Pink glistenings on their heart,
Wide-spread society's flounces,
  The orchard's uncaptured art—
For the bumble-bee band is humming.

  Señor Lark has sung first solo,
    "Where did it reach?" and low
  The breezes stammer, breathless :
    "Only the lark doth know"—
And the clouds are pale with that echo.

  Miss Hawthorne in *grand tier* boxes,
    Peeps, pink,—a glance over there,
  She sees her colors are burning :
    Mr. Robin's *boutonnière!*
And the bumble-bee band is humming.

Now Baritone Bobolink's roulade
Is met with a rain of cheers,
The star-flowers' eyes grow misty,
The buttercups hide their tears,
And the bumble-bee band is sobbing!

Intermezzo. Full-dress ladies
Salute (Eden's manners fine),
Their powdered heads bend together
As if they were taking wine—
And the bumble-bee band is drinking.

But once more a solo maddens—
"Where did it reach!" and low
The Orchard whispers, trembling:
"Only the lark doth know."
But a world is held with that echo!

Robin's New Song.

TILTING on the hawthorne
   White, with love of May,
Robin climbs his ladder:
   Ladder-trills of lay;
Brown beak dipped in summer,
   Heart as red as rose,
Bud that on her lattice
   In the May-breeze blows.

At her lattice-window
   Where the linnet builds,
Where the vines are glistening
   In the dawn's sun-rills,
Waits my ladye Wynneth
   Fair as dawn's pale flush

When the sun's wild wooing
Wakes a crimson blush.

Robin waits, and watches
   (Ah, that brown eye keen!)
The fair ladye Wynneth
   At the casement's green ;
Slowly through the hedge-rows
   Starred with flecks of sun,
Rides Sir Knight, rides slowly,
   Morn's but just begun !—

Robin ! what's that madness
   In the sudden verse
From thy red heart trembling?
   Song, the larks rehearse.
Robin's caught, and tasted
   Her first kiss, above,
Tossed from casement-window,
   Her first kiss of love !

The Fountain.

From the Arabic.

AFAR, I behold the silver sheen
Of the white rose rise o'er the garden's
queens
Like thy moonlight-self o'er the Torrid, love.
Hastening, I hear the white rose speak,
Lulling like leaves of thy moonlight-voice
When thy lips o'erpetal my parched lips, love.

The White Rose.

ON that first blush of Eden
   When the moon looked in
At the love-glow of the garden
   Burned his gaze to win
Love like that deep of Heaven
   When the moon looked in.

On two unfolding rose-lips
   When the moon looked in
Stayed his ivory light, infolding,
   "All thy life I win!"
White is the rose forever,
   For the moon looked in.

The Lightning.

TOWARDS the moon's cruse it leaps,
        it bends and drinks,
And, quaffing heaven, desire
        with distance links.

The Night-Blooming Cereus.

THE stars are out and the green-lipped moon
    in shroud.
The wind that's knocking, soul, at thy door?
Along the marge the moan of the sea,
Circumference of spheric agony,
    What knell is knocking, soul, o'er and o'er?
The world is out in wake of the skeleton cloud.

Thy Hope is out, soul, hell is a-lit and a-leap.
God over gods of hell * * * my white face in
    their deep?

On a branch of the world a silver star!
    A flake from the foam that the moonbeams are
    As they crawl into cadence over the bar
That's haunted with shriek of lost souls afar?

God over gods of hell * * * my white face
   that they reap !

On a branch of the world a silver star !
   From pavement untrodden but by God,
   Glassing, alone, the great antiphons,
   Petal on petal, pearled, spheric tones
   That wake from the opal word of God ;

On a branch of the world a silver star
   Tingèd with angels !—not far, not far !

On a branch of the world a silver star,
   Soul of my soul * * * in this cosmic war
   Wrenched, beckoned, wreathed, a door that's
      ajar
   For the yellow laugh of devils that are—
   Soul of my soul, in thy whitening fight
   Ponder it, down on thy knees to-night

As the devil's dice rattles farther, a-far,
Falls through the black for the nations' toss—
    that's war—

  Soul, that art gripping on God to-night,
On a branch of thy world this silver star
    Tingèd with angels—not far, not far—
    Upbreathes their song-sea, its enringing God,
    A word in the wake of His step star-shod!

Centripetal.

REVERENCE for the atom, dew-drop,
   Shaping self in spheric order,
Reverence for the soul begetteth,
For that supreme work, God's Human :
Dawn of Eden on the forehead,
Dawn of self's august revealments,
"God's own Infinite within me,
Destiny swings in her portals
To my will." The ages prove it.
Once, in wing-sweep o'er the Azure,
It is said the grave archangels
Held the hand a frolic cherub
Stretched towards a drop of fire-mist,
Golden dew-light down the pathways
Constellations tread. The cherub
Stretched his hand towards the sparkle :

"Little ball! a game! I'll toss it!"
Leaped the word of lit archangel:
"Son! Hold thy hand! And kneel!—*The
Earth!*"

The Mayflower.

A MELLOW delight is the meadow
      Mad with May,
Through the green heave the wind's
      Singing its way,
Unfolding and blowing
      In riot and roam
On hedge-row and hill-top
      Its silvering foam,
Through tint and through patter of summer
  shower,
      Mayflower!

A-dream was the Blue of the midnight,
      Dream of Day,
Through the Star-weave the gold's
      Mirrored in May.

Upholding its tapers
    Of light on the land
The buttercups glister
    On violet strand,
Through rose of the sunset and rhyme of shower,
    Star-flower!

A-dream was the nebulous ocean
    One gray Day.
Through the green heave a ship's
    Ploughing its way,
Painting the Infinite
    With soul-prompted star,
A sail 'gainst God's azure
    Grows over the bar!

O'er rocks and o'er storm-beat one crystal comes,
The blossom whose hues are a nations' homes:
    Mayflower!

June.

DAWN of her tangled strains
    May-breezes babbled of through flushing
      lanes ;
    Day of her harmony,
Heaven bending deep: "Thy warm, sweet
      eyes for me ;"
    Night of her bloom, moon-led,
June lifteth up her lips, a rose, love-fed.

Pour Elle.

Cupidon s'asseyait
　　Dans un jardin de pensées,
De son aile plante une plume :
　　"Petit arbre pour l'enchanter !"

Her Girdle.

IT is an orbit in whose zone a star,
   Her woven heart-beats' tune,
Moves with the melody of gods afar
   In permanence of June.

Her Girdle Unclasped.

A S when a goddess turns the lock
    On her illumined lands of night,
The traveller worn for one sweet rest
    Gleaming afar, like Naiad-light
On waters chiming with death's clock—
    Sees haven! through moon-dawn of her
    breast.

A Rose.

A BREATH of God's summer,
O crimsoning new-comer
Whom mortals call a rose?
A spirit-plumed maiden,
A moment pulse-laden
With heaven's red lip that blows.

The Poet's Winnings.

A S THOUGHT by thought drops like the
silver's seven
On rosary, along the poet's vision,
He kneels and listens still within the Elysian
Where roses rhyme their lyric breath with
Heaven.

The Karnak Lily.

D OWN the colossal majesty
 Of Karnak's road I rove,
Pillared on splendor loom the forms
 Of gods, the Theban Jove,
The sacrifice, the mystic rite—
 Vague hieroglyphs of heaven
Foreshadowing ecstacy beyond
 The sacred columns seven.
The vocal glooms of solitude,
 The thunderous silence speaks,
The roll of ages mounts,—its voice
 The soul of man. It seeks
Some boon from awful Amon-Ra:
 "To me, thou Sun-god, come!"
The shadows sweep the solitudes,

The fervent lips are dumb.

    *   *   *   *

On the still breast of Heaven's blue,
  Anchored in seas of light,
Crown of the column's majesty,
  The lotus floats in sight,
The lotus-lily to the sun
  Lifts lip, and has the god's kiss won!

The Egyptian Obelisk.

I

STERN staying Index on the clanging turn
Of dappled Time, pointing to One—man's
bourn.

.

The Egyptian Obelisk.

II

WHAT word of old stayed thy bright bound
        towards firmaments of One,
Thou mystic fount from fathomless,
        thou Prism of the sun!

Révélé.

Je monte, et je vois
   Sur les ailes de l' Amour
L'horizon qui se cache
   Pour les autres en plein jour.

For Whom?

THE misted moon had bared her breast.
  The star-strong steel of warriors seven
Anointed in the sunset's crest,
  Waits maddened, trembling on Heaven's rim.
    Her smiling tips
With *fleur-de-lis* their lance.   Still dim,
    Unquaffed those lips,
They wildly stare upon Madonna-maid in Heaven.

Transfiguration.

I.

THE sacred raiment I put off
    So soon her smile hath gone
That clothed me with that clime that holds
    The deathless rose of dawn.

Transfiguration.

II.

SHE comes, my lady comes.
   I tremble, I, a man.
Yet when her lips cross my soul's sill, I
   Know what Immortals can!

One Moonlight.

From the Persian.

HE kissed a crescent on my lips,
  Half-circle sweet, if small,
It burns a Heaven upon the night—
  It holds an Orient's All.

A Prayer.

SAY ye one word down the dread silences,
 O angels great of God who bend and lift
Those murmurous vesture-folds of Time
Whose voices stir from out an Infinite;
And give to soul, not sense, one thrill of Him
The Word, who waits within the Eternal Veil
With eyes intent upon our manhood's life
In all its leap and lift, its strife, its storm,
Its currents counting slow through the great dark
To that lit Vast whose stars are harbor-lights.
On manhood's pulse with all its possible,
Lift, messengers of God, one thrill of Him
Whose eyes are vistas of man's ultimate—
 For lo, in His, our veins do rhyme!

A Meeting.*

HE stands to-day upon the street,
  The Infinite street of many lights,
Shadows have sunk into the night—
  Shadows, and the Four Hundred lights.

Silence along the Infinite Street—
  The burning gaze of the Expanse
Bends but one way; upon two men
  Who meet. There's silence in the advance.

Of moments in the Eternal Day
  ("Good Form" obtains in highest Heaven),
One of these men is speaking, see!
  A hush through the great Trumpets seven.

* One of Mr. M⁻Allister's maxims is said to have been : "*If you see a man with a shabby coat, cross the street to avoid him.*"

He stands upon the Eternal Street
Of wide-ascending, argent light,
A dazzle "Patriarchs" never dreamed,
Nor Prophets, nor a Pope in white.

He stands upon the Eternal Street,
The radiance is of hue unpriced—
What form is this that faces him?
The poor storm-shattered serge of Christ;

The Man who wore the "shabby coat"
For the long space of heavy years
For this man, all men. Once, cast out
By a "Four Hundred's" cultured sneers.

What canst thou do, O soul? Decide!
He faces thee, the Nazarene.
Thou canst not "cross" the Eternal Street,
Thou canst not shirk that Face once seen.

www.ingramcontent.com/pod-product-compliance
Lightning Source LLC
Chambersburg PA
CBHW030610270326
41927CB00007B/1115